Sketchbook

This book belongs to

Emily

Sunglasses!

Made in the USA
San Bernardino, CA
19 December 2019

61990464R00058